DANCING IN THE CLOUD

Krystle -

You are a fire starter for
Jesus, the Lord will
continue to use you
mightly, may you
behold the beauty
of Jesus everyday
and turn your attention
to Him - A quiet heart
beating unto God is
the highest form of
prayer, so let your
heart beat to His
beauty in stillness

— Love
Chris

ISBN-13: 9798634707648

A Publication of Tall Pine Books
|| tallpinebooks.com

DANCING IN THE CLOUD

DISCOVERING THE PLACE WE GET LOST IN

CHRIS DIXON

Tall Pine

AUTHOR'S NOTE

This book was inspired by a man from Switzerland who was at the Jesus 2019 Conference in Orlando, Florida. He told me the Lord has called me "in the cloud," and this is how I got the title of my book.

Poems by Chris Dixon, featuring Madelyn Badillo

CONTENTS

Dressed in all white
I see my Bride Groom King
His presence so bright
Shining brighter than a diamond ring
Heart-shaped eyes with wings
The lover of my soul, my everything

Crown on His head
Holes in His hands and feet
He is the daily bread
That I eat

The irresistible Christ
The One who bled for me
The perfect sacrifice
The One who set me free

Slipping in His sweet presence
I am lifted into the Heavens
In the cloud of His essence
Raptured in seconds

I am dancing in the cloud
My Beloved looks so proud
And with angels singing out loud
He gives me a crown

Today He who hung the earth upon the waters is hung on a tree. The King of the angels is decked with a crown of thorns. He who wraps the heavens in clouds is wrapped in the purple of mockery. He who freed Adam in the Jordan is slapped in the face. The Bridegroom of the Church is affixed to the cross with nails. The Son of the Virgin is pierced by a spear. We worship Thy passion, O Christ. Show us also Thy glorious resurrection.

He who clothes Himself with light as with a garment stood naked for trial. He was struck on the cheek by hands that He himself had formed. A people that transgressed the law nailed the Lord of Glory to the cross.

Then the curtain of the temple was torn in two. Then the

sun was darkened, Unable to bear the sight of God outraged, Before Whom all things tremble. Let us worship Him.

The disciples denied Him, But the thief cried out: "Remember me, O Lord, in Thy Kingdom!"

This book is dedicated to Jesus, my Bridegroom King. Thank You for encountering me with Your love and beauty. Thank You for saving me. You are everything to me. I love dancing in front of the throne room of Your heart and feeling Your sweet presence. The intimate times we shared together as I dance or just sit at Your feet, the ocean depths of Your love have forever wrecked me to fall in love with You more every day. I am lovesick for You, O God. You are enough for me, for eternity. I love you forever!

First and foremost, I want to thank my mother. You are my best friend. From the beginning you have been my number one supporter in my dance gift. You always enjoy watching me dance. And I enjoy spending time with you. I am grateful that God chose you to be my mom and me to be your son.

To my grandmother, thank you for your help in raising me. I enjoyed your cooking, the times we went to church together, and especially seeing you living your life loving Jesus. I will forever miss you, and I will see you one day in Heaven.

To my brother Jeff, thanks for being there for me when my dad wasn't around and for believing in me. The parties you DJ'ed were my springboard into my dancing journey.

Thank you to my sister Danielle and my brother-in-law Chad for introducing me to Jesus and sharing the gospel with me. You gave me my first study Bible with my name on it, and it was the best gift anyone could have given me. You both saw purpose, potential, and destiny in me to live for God, and I am extremely humbled and grateful for you both.

I would like to mention of a couple of people that have greatly impacted and challenged me with their teaching to go deeper in my intimate relationship with the Lord. Thank you, Eric Gilmour of Sonship International and Pastor Dan Mohler of Neck Ministries.

Thank you, Pastors Denise and David Greco for all your encouraging words uplifting my spirit. You have both been a huge blessing in my life and have grounded me in the Word of God. You have been great supporters of my gift of dance the Lord has given me to bless others. I love and honor you with all of my heart.

To Pastor George Searight II, I love and appreciate you brother; you are truly anointed preaching the gospel and creative using visual presentations. Every time I see you, you are always dressed in style. Thanks for always encouraging me in my life pointing me to honor the Lord with my creative art in dance and film.

To Ali Ferrell, I am beyond thankful for you, for giving me room at the House of Prayer "Resting Place" to worship God, have fellowship with others, and dance to Jesus. I call this place home. You have encouraged me when I wanted to give up and never let me stay where I was. You called me higher and spoke in my life that God would never leave me and He is always with me. I love you, bro.

Thank you, Shanai, for being a vessel of honor and grace as the leader of our dance team at Resting Place House of Prayer.

To my best friend Q, I appreciate you, bro. If it wasn't for you, I wouldn't be dancing for the Lord today. Thank you for allowing God to use you and for inviting me to your church.

To Geo Hubela, Thank you for believing in me since day one. As my first Hip Hop teacher, I learned a great deal from you. I started not knowing how to do choreography, and you instructed me how to execute it with precision. It was a blessing being on Team USA for the IDO World Hip Hop Dance Championship in Bremerhaven, Germany, with you as my coach; you were remarkable! This was an inspirational learning opportunity, which was for me as a dancer, competing against different countries around the globe representing Team USA, an unforgettable highlight of my life. I also want to thank you for making it possible for me to teach dance weekly at your studio ICON. I love teaching and inspiring the kids, it's one of the best feelings in the world. I now understand why you love what you do. I appreciate and value you. Never stop dancing.

To Kevin Paradox, Thank you for your passion and creativity in the art of dance. I have enjoyed watching all of your "Ask a Paradox Series" on YouTube, and they have inspired me on so many levels in my own dance journey and life in general. I also enjoyed participating in your 30 days of dance on Instagram, which propelled me to push myself to improve my dance. In my opinion your theory of movement is remarkable and quite genius. Hands down, you are my favorite dancer. Your "Life of a tree" dance video was the most beautiful piece of art I have ever seen in my life. Every time I watch you dance, I do not just see a dancer; I see a brilliant artist. Keep growing and inspiring the world with your beautiful craft.

To my spiritual momma Luz, thank you for always being there when I needed someone to talk to. The Lord has used you in supernatural ways to just say the right things, always point me to Jesus, and have intimacy with Him above all.

To Wally, thanks for being there for me. You have kept me accountable to the Lord and have spoken in my life countless of times. I appreciate the Lord putting you in my life. And the moments hanging out was always a creative adventure.

And to the rest of my family in God, you all have encouraged me and inspired me on so many levels, in so many ways, and you are all truly a gift from God that I do not take for granted. I deeply love you all from the bottom of my heart.

1 / DANCE IS ART

"Dance is the art of the soul painted on the canvas of life."

- *KEVIN PARADOX*

I STARTED DANCING 19 YEARS AGO. EVEN THOUGH I BEGAN WITH Hip Hop Choreography, I became more and more passionate for freestyle dancing as time went by. I fell in love with making art with my body, and I wanted to reach the highest level of artistry through my movement and see how far I could reach. So, I practiced consistently to refine my movement.

The styles of dance I learned were popping, locking, animation, and krump. I grew up watching NSYNC, Backstreet Boys, Michael Jackson, Chris Brown, and Usher. Every time I saw Usher glide, it mesmerized me and I was compelled to learn this move, so I would practice on my kitchen floor or outside. I remember watching from Soul Train and seeing the Electric Boogaloos and the Lockers; these amazing individuals were my inspiration to dance. I learned watching them on YouTube. One of my huge inspirations was Steffan "Mr. Wiggles" Clemente from Rock Steady Crew and the Electric Boogaloos. I would order his DVDs online and watch them to learn popping, and I would practice in my living room. I really enjoyed making dance videos for my own YouTube channel and sharing my art with the world. The world was my canvas and my body was the paint brush; I wanted to leave my sketch on the earth through dance. On chill days, I would turn up the music in my room and dance for hours. I just wanted to keep getting better and improve myself.

I have had the blessing to dance around the U.S. and in many different countries. Traveling has helped me open up my mind for creativity and expand my movement by learning from different individuals and cultures in their uniqueness. Dancing has taught me to cherish every moment through the journey, and failure has not been the end but a stepping stone for me to grow. Furthermore, I have learned patience as I have taken time and not rushed through the process as I have learned new styles or improved by existing ones.

To dance is to speak without saying a word, touching

people's lives with the sketch of my gifts and drawing them to experience the message being released through every movement. Dance is a language that can be understood worldwide regardless of the spoken language. It is a gift every individual can enjoy in their own uniqueness.

In one of his Youtube videos, Kevin Paradox expressed his belief that music is creation. He went on to say that everything in this world has a rhythm, everything. The sun and the moon have a certain rhythm. The way the earth rotates has a rhythm, the way we wake up and go back to bed, the way we eat, the way our heart beats, the way we walk - everything has a rhythm. This universe is created of rhythms and actually music. All we do as dancers is embody the patterns we see in this world in our own different ways: emotions, life experience, colors, and thoughts. It's a guide for us to understand certain things in our life. In my opinion, Paradox's explanation is key to all dancers; I'm blown away by it.

Dance is like a huge painting using life itself as its canvas, which operates wherever we dance. The human body is its brush, which uses the colors represented by the dancing techniques. If we only have one color "splat", and we only paint the tree with one color, the water with one color and so on, then the painting is not going to be diverse; we are not going to be able to create whatever we picture in our minds and what we feel. Therefore, we need a myriad of colors to be able to create detailed pictures of our soul with our body. Furthermore, it is to our advantage to learn as many techniques as possible and become a part of a growing and evolving world of dance as an art expression.

I am rare
To sketch the air

The Lord has anointed me
To dance creatively

And express art
That flows from the depths of my heart

The brush of my fingers
In His presence lingers

When I begin to dance from my soul
I lose all control

The beauty of my movement
Is dancing in communion

With Jesus
The one who frees us

2 / RAISED UP IN RELIGION

"This is the heart of the spirit of religion: 'Give them everything but His presence.' Why? Because only His presence gives life. This is why some hate religion and why others die under it, because it only gives a picture of Jesus but never introduces the person of Jesus."

- ERIC GILMOUR

WHEN I WAS A YOUNG BOY, MY GRANDMOTHER BROUGHT ME TO A catholic church frequently on Sundays. She loved Jesus and I always saw her praying with her rosary beads in her room. At church, as I sat down next to my grandma, the beautiful sounds of hymns heard through the piano created an atmosphere of holiness.

Unfortunately, the priest preaching was hard to under-stand; and it became more uncomfortable after kneeling for an extended period of time. Thoughts ran through my mind, why did we have to do this instead of sitting down? But I wanted to honor my grandmother, so I did what she asked.

My grandmother explained to me about communion. She told me that if I wanted to be cleansed from my sins, to go up in the line and eat the bread and drink the wine. The bread repre-sented the broken body of Jesus. The wine represented His blood that poured out. The bread tasted like sandpaper and the wine tasted like sour grape juice.

Some Sundays, I was told by the minister to confess my sins to him so God would forgive me. I did this frequently. It was pretty weird being in a closed boxed room with him behind a gated door hearing my confessions and me being on the other side.

I never knew if I was good enough for God. Years went by and I was extremely bored. Church had become mundane for me, but I went to keep my grandmother happy. I remember going with my mom and my brother every year on special holi-days like Christmas Eve. I knew as a young boy that there had to be more to church. How can someone like me have a rela-tionship with this God that felt so distant? I didn't feel His pres-ence in the service. As I got older and didn't notice any change of greater intimacy with the God that was being preached, I concluded that church wasn't for me.

I asked my mom one day in my room, "Am I a good person to go to Heaven?" She said, "Well, of course! Just do your Our

Father and Hail Mary prayers every day." So, I did. Kneeling on the rug and my head on my bed, I prayed every night. This had me thinking that I was a good person and that I would make it to Heaven; all I needed to do was pray and believe.

Going through the motions of religion

Was a conscious decision

Every Sunday I would drown in my own thoughts
Hymns, prayer, sermon, and I still felt lost

Is this really it?
Stand, kneel, and sit

I was bored out my mind
Hopeless and blind

My worship to God was lifeless
No matter what I did I never felt righteous

Didn't feel His presence
Never thought I would make it to Heaven

Good works didn't save me
I needed the living Christ to live in me

And then I heard about Jesus Christ,
That He is the perfect sacrifice

And I knew that He was what was missing in my life
He opened up my eyes
And reassured me that He, the living God heard my cry

So I went from knowing about Him
To being known by Him

No longer going through the motions of religion
But walking in the freedom that He's given
Surrendering my life to Jesus was the best decision

3 / TORMENT

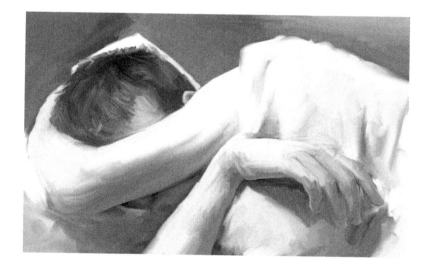

"*Nothing in this world will torment you as much as your own thoughts.*"

- *ALI B. MOE*

.

IN MY EARLY TEENAGE YEARS, I SUFFERED WITH DEPRESSION, anxiety, suicidal thoughts, and loneliness. I used dance to medicate myself so that I wouldn't feel the pain of what I was going through. Dance was my escape to freedom. When I didn't want to be home on weekends and was old enough, I would go to the clubs to dance. That's when I started meeting a lot of pretty girls and dancing was my net to catch them; they loved the way I danced and that gave me the sign to pursue them. I needed to feel loved, and I was addicted to the lifestyle of sexual immorality.

During the nights, I would get horrific demonic dreams. I would see black shadows in my room coming over me while I was sleeping. I couldn't move or talk. I was scared. I didn't know why this was happening to me. These lucid dreams would happen frequently, and they were not stopping.

One day I told my friend Syed of my nightmarish experiences, and he took me to the Catholic church where my grandmother had taken me before. We both talked with the priest, and he explained that the spiritual realm was real and that I was seeing demons. He gave me holy water to sprinkle in my room. I did as he said, but that didn't stop the nightmares. However, the thought of the name of Jesus rose within me and I would say the name, and the demons would flee. Yet the dreams of hell and being tortured would return.

In one of my dreams, I was taking out a black rope from my mouth; it looked like dark blood and the rope would never end. I was looking for peace, so I would go into meditation called Astral Projection, which is described to be an intentional out of body experience. I tried and tried, but nothing worked.

While visiting my brother down the shore, there was a Java Joint and in it there was a psychic who only charged 10 dollars for a spiritual reading. I thought to myself that I needed to know about my future. With her tarot cards, she would give me spiritual readings of my life. But she never mentioned the word

"Jesus" to me, not even once. Some things she said were true; others were not. Yet, I visited her on a regular basis for about a year with my mother and grandmother. I started reading my horoscopes online to know more about myself and my purpose. I didn't realize I was going deeper and deeper into darkness, headed to hell.

The darkness in my soul
Was as black as coal

I had no purpose
Living like a breathing carcass

Dancing was my medication
Not just my occupation

I was addicted to girls
From all parts of the world

Sex was my way of coping
Leaving others like me, broken

Demonic dreams in a cycle
I was going down a spiral

Seeing demons before my very eyes
I felt like I was going to die

Everything around me was toxic
My mind was chaotic

Thoughts ripped me apart
Torment is an ancient art
But Jesus conquered it before the start

4 / FIRST ENCOUNTER

"No past is dark enough to withstand a transforming encounter with God."

- JARRID WILSON

I was invited to a Christian church by one of my best friends, Adquil Lee. We danced in the clubs over a decade together, and he told me one day that he is a minister and a dancer for God. I was blown away even though I couldn't comprehend what he was trying to say. At his church, I saw people encountering God for the first time; it was unreal! I remember seeing this on YouTube, but never in person. The pastor asked if anyone needed prayer, so I went up nervously and the pastor anointed my head with oil and prayed for me. I felt the touch of God for the first time and fell to the floor. Then every week, I wanted to get prayed for by him just to experience God in that special way.

Adquil asked me one day to come over his house for his sister's baby shower; we ate and fellowshipped. I asked Adquil if I could dance and he said sure. My pastor was there and saw me dance, and he thought it was demonic because he had never seen someone dance for the Lord in that way.

One Sunday morning, I saw a flyer for a youth gathering at my church and wanted to dance. I love performing in front of crowds and have been doing it for a very long time, but never in church before. In my upbringing, I never saw dancing in church. That night, I asked my pastor if I could dance, and he asked me to see him in the back of the church. He wanted to ask me what song I wanted to dance to, so I told him, "Hillsong - Glorious Ruins." He was very skeptical of what I was going to do because he knew I didn't do regular praise dancing that looked more contemporary. He remembered what he thought when he first saw me dance at my friend's backyard. Yet he told me I could minister through dance and gave me a chance. So, I rushed to my car and popped out my Hillsong CD and brought it to be played.

As I began to dance, I waved my arms and glided across the floor. I began to feel lost in time and a peace rushed through my body; I was moved to tears. This never happened to me before. I was feeling God's presence and His love for the first time through movement. People were shouting and praising the Lord watching me dance and God got all the glory. I was wrecked by God's presence that night. The kids loved it, and the pastor felt the Holy Spirit's presence as he looked into my eyes.

I then heard in my spirit coming from the throne of Heaven, "I have given you the gift to dance, now don't waste it but use it around the world." This first encounter changed my life forever, and I decided to give my life to Jesus and be a Christian.

"A man's gift makes room for him, and brings him before great men."—Proverbs 18:16

So I started to dance at open mics and different churches all over New Jersey, New York, and Pennsylvania. God opened the doors for me to dance at the Legendary Apollo Stage and I got to minister through dance to the songs "What Can I Do" by Tye Tribbett and "Break Every Chain" by Tasha Cobbs. It was so powerful, not because of what I did, but because of how God danced through me, and the crowds were touched. After this, I was able to travel around the world and minister before the Lord.

I remember that moment in time
In which the God of the Universe
Immersed me in His presence

I remember how in a matter of seconds
My life was transformed by His acceptance of me
As I danced, He poured out His love
and revealed to me who I was meant to be

One sentence provided a lifetime of refreshing
and blessing, for now I was connected to heaven

That first encounter changed everything
now I live and dance for the King
Who met me at my lowest point
with a robe and a ring

5 / THE SECRET PLACE

"Could there be anything more important than sitting in silence before God every day?"

- **A.W. TOZER**

IN MY DILIGENT PURSUIT OF KNOWING GOD, I HAVE COME TO realize that to intimately know Jesus and become more like Him is the highest priority in my life. As I seek His face daily, I am learning more and more to fall madly in love with Him. There is no greater accomplishment in my life than be consumed by His presence. And as this relationship deepens, I'm experiencing new levels of joy and freedom in Him. He is my greatest pleasure on this earth. My destiny is in His hands, and I want to partner with Him to see my purpose in Him come true.

His presence and voice come hand and hand; I wouldn't be able to hear His voice if I wasn't in His presence. Moses had to turn to the fiery bush and give God his attention for him to hear God speak. So, I must give all my attention to Him and adore Him. He brands me every day through our vertical encounters. The hinge upon my life is Jesus; I must not let go but always hold on.

I know busyness comes in life and I must turn my gaze. I have learned that I spend my time and focus on whatever my priority in life is. The greatest priority should be intimately loving Him and loving Him well. My passion is Jesus. I can now dance for Him and give the Lord all the glory. He rewards me for seeking Him in the secret place. According to Eric Gilmour the secret place is the presence of the Lord. It is not just a physical location; it is a state of being in union and consciousness of God's presence.

He is the Bridegroom King and I am the Bride. Imagine a bride and groom that never spend time with each other; that wouldn't be much of a relationship. So, it is my love that I be with Him. I must wait on the Lord daily, be silent, yield to Him so that I can hear His voice. I feel His tangible touch in my hands when I am in His presence. All the rooms of my heart are filled. Every day I want to know Him more.

"My beloved is mine, and I am his. —Song of Solomon 2:16 (NKJV)

"Because you are close to me and always available, my confidence will never be shaken, for I experience your wrap-around presence every moment." —Psalm 16:8

When I give God my affection and adoration, there is an eruption of love that comes up from my heart. Seeing Jesus and beholding His glory is the only way to be transformed into the image of Jesus. Time alone with Him is number ONE.

"Be still, and know that I am God! —Psalm 46:10 (NLT)

Rest is not just a vacation; rest is Him. External noise can be around me and I can go somewhere to be quiet, but the internal noise no matter where I am is only still when I come to Him. So, let's make it our lifestyle to be at the feet of Jesus, addicted to His presence all the days of our lives in the secret place.

The secret place
Is where I lay my face

Where I fall in love over and over again
The place where He calls me friend

He is my greatest pleasure
My only treasure

The creative expression of my existence
Longs for His appearance

To see the Bride Groom King
For all eternity I will dance and sing

I give Him day and night devotion
He has all my thoughts and all my emotions

Busyness tries to come in
But I always must sit to be with Him

Waiting on the Lord daily
Even when I feel lazy

David never stopped gazing

Because God's love is so amazing

To dwell in the House of the Lord
Is bigger than any reward

Beholding His glory
I have set the Lord always before me

This is the place where I give God my very best
And come to Him to give me rest

The place where I lay my life down
And daily contend for a heavenly crown

"We find rest in those we love, and we provide a resting place in ourselves for those who love us."

– *SAINT BERNARD OF CLAIRVAUX*

I HAVE BEEN ATTENDING RESTING PLACE HOUSE OF PRAYER FOR about 7 years, and it has changed my life. God has encountered and wrecked me with His love hundreds of times by just adoring Him in this special place. Many times, when the worship starts, the instruments begin to prophesy, and the voices join in one accord to sing praises to the King, I close my eyes and just see Him. I sense the Holy Spirit caress my face and hands as I dance before the Lord with all my strength. I weep before Him, sensing His presence. I hear people worshipping the Lord, singing unto Him as if they were angels in Heaven. My eyes begin to open and I see dancers on stage dancing and pouring out their incense to the Lord.

The time came when the Lord made it clear that He was calling me to be on the praise dance team and minister to others. So, I obeyed the voice of the Lord and joined. On selected nights each week, I poured all my love out through my body and was story-telling through movement. It was so beautiful to express myself and dance for God's glory. There were times when a couple of us on stage were doing choreography and it felt as if we were in one accord, dancing to our Heavenly Father. I have seen the atmosphere in the room change a lot of times when we have danced, and everybody joined in and started to dance like David. It was so beautiful! I didn't just see dancers on stage but dancers who flag; these flags had different colors and meant something prophetic, moving as if they were arms swinging. In the Bible, it talks about the banner of love. And when I see flagging, it reminds me of God's love.

One Monday night, the praise dance team was all dressed in white. There was a sense of supernatural connectivity, as if we were angels on a stage in the throne room of the Holy of Holies. My friends Ianni and Shamma danced with me on stage; we linked arms and connected as one. It was such a beautiful chemistry unto God. I stopped just to adore Jesus and felt the tranquility of the Lord's presence illuminate my being in stillness. People came up to us that night and said we looked like angels dancing in the throne room.

Ali Ferrell, the director of Resting Place, encouraged all the team to dance and prophesy through our movement while the worship team played. It was a heavenly experience that shifted the atmosphere. Rich Monaco, one of the leaders of Resting Place, encouraged everyone present to join in, praying for all the creatives, dancers, writers, musicians, and flaggers. As these were being prayed for, the Lord ministered to them.

There have been many other evenings of amazing encounters of worship while dancing for my King. And with each experience, the Lord has placed a firm belief in my spirit and mind that He will birth the creative arts in all the Houses of Prayer around the world. This will allow His people to worship creatively on earth as the angels do in Heaven.

Underneath my skin
Is the Resting Place that God dwells in

His presence wraps around me
Like water to fish under the sea

I am touched so sweetly
I feel God's love so deeply

There is a Resting Place
where I see people in deep adoration
Looking to Jesus who designed Creation

A face to face encounter
With blessing, honor, glory, and power

The love of Jesus becomes so tangible
As we feel the invisible

Hearts are changing
Like colors on a painting

Lives are being transformed
The Son of God being adored

7 / CREATIVITY

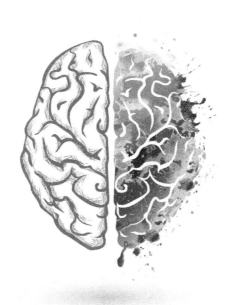

"Creativity is not a mood. Creativity is not a gift. It's the very nature of God inside of you."

- *DAN MCCOLLAM*

CREATIVITY UNLOCKS CHARACTERISTICS OF GOD IN US LIKE nothing else; it goes beyond what words can say. God is the ultimate creative being who makes everything purposeful and majestic with the intention of drawing His perfect creation in mankind to a heart relationship. Creativity is in our DNA. God shows His creation in the book of *Genesis 1:1 which states, "In the beginning God created the Heavens and the earth..."*

> *"Then God said, 'Let Us make man in Our image, according to Our likeness; let them have dominion over the fish of the sea, over the birds of the air, and over the cattle, over all the earth and over every creeping thing that creeps on the earth." So God created man in His own image; in the image of God He created him; male and female He created them. Then God blessed them, and God said to them, "Be fruitful and multiply; fill the earth and subdue it; have dominion over the fish of the sea, over the birds of the air, and over every living thing that moves on the earth.'" —Genesis 1:16-28*

Since we have been made in God's image, then we can believe that we were made to be creative, using the skills and gifts given to us by the Master of Creation. As we yield to our Creator, He brings out our creative talents so that we can, in turn, bless His creation.

Creativity is all about taking risks. When I create something from God's perspective, not only does He delight in this, but He also provides the wisdom to create from His perfect love, which exalts Jesus. As creative beings, our hardships are also used by the Lord to teach us to be compassionate and transform others. As we embrace Jesus in our lives, we are no longer orphans in creativity. Experience with God creates a path for others to follow. We are called to be renaissance men or women, discovering new expressions of beauty and creativity and using them to bring glory to God and to transform our world. The beauty of creativity has the capacity to carry what cannot be carried in other ways, arguments, or politics. Expressions can be stated from art and creativity that cannot be challenged in any other way.

What I do is actually a tool of creativity, like a vehicle I can use to communicate to the world. I believe we are entering into a creative age in this year, 2020, that we have not experienced in the past. God wants us to exercise creativity on this side of eternity. We need to start training our imagination to think outwardly, expressing the quality of the Maker that has made us to be creative. We are not here on earth to just pay our bills but also to imagine and create something new into the world individually. The very fact that we can create something is a statement of faith. If you are faithful to your craft and diligently expanding your creativity and imagination, God will honor that. We must be the aroma of Christ in a dying world. Let's be a people that live in freedom to be fearless, especially in creativity. Ask the Holy Spirt what to say, what to do, where to go, and what to create.

Isaiah 14:12-17 (NKJV) states, "How you are fallen from heaven, O Lucifer, son of the morning! How you are cut down to the ground, You who weakened the nations! For you have said in your heart; I will ascent into heaven, I will exalt my throne above the stars of God; I will also sit on the mount of the congregation on the farthest sides of the north; I will ascend above the heights of the clouds, I will be like the Most High. Yet you shall be brought down to Sheol, to the lowest depths of the Pit. Those who see you will gaze at you, And consider you, saying: Is this the man who made the earth tremble, Who shook kingdoms, Who made the world as a wilderness and destroyed its cities, Who did not open the house of his prisoners?"

When Lucifer fell, so did his beauty. His greatest pursuit has been to deceive mankind to fall, as well. Because of this, people worship the created instead of the Creator. Furthermore, their creativity and beauty are tainted without real transformation from the Creator.

"Believe in me so that rivers of living water will burst out from within you, flowing from your innermost being, just like the Scripture says!" —*John 7:38*

"Have you forgotten that your body is now the sacred temple of the Spirit of Holiness, who lives in you? You don't belong to yourself any longer, for the gift of God, the Holy Spirit, lives inside your sanctuary. You were God's expensive purchase, paid for with tears of blood, so by all means, then, use your body to bring glory to God!" —*1 Corinthians 6:19-20*

Beauty through creativity is a gift from God to mankind and has a double assignment: to point mankind to God and to carry truth to the world.

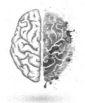

Creating in silence
I make things in His presence

My imagination is tailor-made
For my art to be displayed

Reflecting to the One true Artist
His light shines in the darkness

Creating within space and time
Everything He made is defined

When we collaborate
We appreciate

From one artist to another
Let us inspire each other

Creating in silence
Let us make things in His presence

That display the beauty and glory
of the only One found worthy

"Israel was not created in order to disappear; Israel will endure and flourish."

— *JOHN F. KENNEDY*

I REMEMBER IT AS IF IT WAS YESTERDAY. I WAS AT RESTING PLACE House of Prayer in New Jersey, and it was such an intimate night worshipping the Lord. I was dancing next to a light stand and my eyes were closed; I was gazing at the Lord, sweat coming down my face, my body feeling hot. I was in God's presence and felt like time didn't exist, it was just Him and me. All of a sudden, I felt a tap on my shoulder as I was dancing, but I didn't know who it was because my eyes were still closed. I heard a small voice of a woman saying in my ear, "The Lord is bringing you to Israel. You are going to dance on the streets of gold like King David did." Once I heard that, I began to weep; I felt the presence of the Lord even more strongly. The Lord put it on her and her husband's heart to sponsor me and pay for the whole trip. That was such a blessing from God. I knew then that when the Lord calls you to a specific place, He would make a way and provide.

Months later the trip became a reality. For a whole week, I toured the Holy Land with the ministry Christ For All Nations led by Daniel Kolenda. A highlight of the trip was a day we got to be on a boat sailing the Sea of Galilee. The experience was majestic; we had wonderful worship on the boat as the sun glistened on the water. I knew I needed to take this once-in-a-lifetime opportunity to dance on the boat, so as everyone was singing worship songs, I was dancing as the cool breeze hit my face. I could not believe I was dancing on the Sea of Galilee where Jesus walked. It felt like a dream come true.

Days later, as I walked the streets of Jerusalem, I saw some Jewish guys playing music, so I decided to join in and dance to the sound of the music. I then noticed a girl dancing nearby, and I asked her to join me. We had a special moment and it seemed more like a divine appointment. It reminded me of The Bridegroom King dancing with His Bride.

After the dance, I toured the rest of Jerusalem. Toward the end of the trip, I got to visit The Garden Tomb where Jesus laid long ago. I stepped inside the Garden Tomb and began to weep; the presence of God was so thick and tangible. I had ten minutes in the Tomb and it felt like I was in Heaven, singing to Him with my whole heart. When I came out of the Tomb, I was compelled to dance in front of it, and time seemed eternal during those few moments that I will never forget. Michael Aviel has once said, "When He comes into our hearts—the state of the heart is that of the tomb in which He was buried." I believe "My body is a tomb in which God walks through every time I dance." So in newness of life He kisses the heart to life.

Israel is the most beautiful place on earth
This is where Mary gave birth

Jesus the Son of God being born
And the veil being torn

Where He died to wash our sins away
And resurrected on the third day

I see Him looking at me
As I dance on the Sea of Galilee

I feel His sweet presence
The waters turn iridescent

I hear music in the streets of Jerusalem
The musicians are in unison

I dance on the streets
that carry the story of all that He's done

Israel where He first gave of Himself
so that we could be one

"California is an unbelievable state."

— *DREW BARRYMORE*

THE INSPIRATION TO MOVE TO CALIFORNIA CAME FROM THE BOOK, *The Artisan Soul*, by Erwin Raphael MacManus. In a summary of the book it states, "If this book is of any value at all, it is my hope that you will once again see yourself through the eyes of a child, or at the very least see that you, too, were no ordinary child — that you are, in fact, divine material.

"Just as the Lord God told Jeremiah that before he was born he knew him and while he was still in his mother's womb he called him out, this same truth applies to you. In the full meaning of the word, you were born a masterpiece, a work of art, an expression of the divine imagination, but you are both a work of art and an artist at work, and this is why the life you live and the choices you make are critical. We can deny who we are and say that we are not creative, we're not artistic, we're not imaginative, but this doesn't excuse us from our responsibility. You have been given a great gift, and that gift is your life."

This book opened up a passion in my soul to explore and to create in the land where so many people have done so.

In 2018, I ended up moving to California. The plan was to film for my friend's ministry and stay at his home during that time, but the Lord intervened and changed my plans. He was calling me to obedience in learning to listen to His voice and to go on a faith adventure with Him. This meant leaving my friend's place and trusting the Lord for a new place to stay. I looked around for a place but could not find anything. I was becoming discouraged when I heard the Lord say, "If you pack your bags, get back on the plane, and move back to New Jersey, you will be living in disobedience." I then felt the conviction of the Lord rise up within me to stick it out and stay. These two Scriptures spoke to me greatly:

"For we walk by faith, not by sight." —2 Corinthians 5:7

"But seek first the kingdom of God and His righteousness, and all these things shall be added to you." —Matthew 6:33

It seemed as if my life was literally hanging on these Scriptures. At a prophetic meeting, I met Bruce Thompson Jr.; we became friends and he allowed me to stay at his place until I was able to get on my feet. He was compassionate and represented Christ to me as a true brother of the faith.

Later, I called my friend Nathan Dukes, whom I had met in Israel. He had mentioned at that time that he was part of a discipleship school called Ekballo in Pasadena. I was intrigued and interested about this school, so I asked him about attending the school and doing video. He connected me with his leader, Mando Matthews. When I met with Mando, I shared with him about my involvement with Resting Place House of Prayer and Global School of Supernatural Ministry in New York City. I showed him the video work I had done for both of these ministries, and he was impressed. I then spoke of meeting Nathan Dukes in Israel and this was a huge connect since Nathan was a 2nd year student at Ekballo. Mando and I came to the agreement that I would do video and photography work for the school, and that my work would cover the cost of attending the school. I kept my word and did extensive work while I was there. During the year, I learned to be discipled, grew in intimacy with the Lord, and lived with a community of believers four days a week from morning to late afternoon. Monday nights we had fellowship and food at the house.

This program taught me to really walk as a disciple of Jesus and not just a believer in Him. In that season of my life, a hunger stirred in me for the Word of God and I just kept going deeper and deeper. An example of a decision I had to make was to choose to whether to buy a very special Bible called the Revival Study Bible, which costs about $150, or choose to buy two weeks worth of food. I concluded that the Bible was my bread to eat spiritually and I was to feed on the Living Word, so I bought it. A big part of our homework assignments was to read the Word.

A highlight of being a student at Ekballo was the 10pm to 4am prayer in the nights. Each student was assigned specific nights to attend; it was not easy, but we learned to be disciplined and persevere. We would worship the Lord and cry out for revival and pray interceding for California to turn back to God. We had a prayer wall where we wrote on the chalkboard the names of our family and friends and others that we wanted to see come to the Lord and be saved. We prayed for the LGBTQ community and to see a new Jesus People movement arise again. Every week, we were doing outreaches on college campuses, and we saw the Lord breakthrough in people's lives. Some of the most precious times were when we fellowshipped singing worship songs around the bonfire; it was a wonderful time. The presence of God was so tangible. We had these epic worship nights and abiding times with the Lord, and I would just dance my heart out or be still before Him. His presence was sweeter than Starburst candy.

Another special part of my stay with Ekballo happened at the organized worship events where I would share my gift of dance with these amazing talented people that loved Jesus the way I do; it was glorious! I was pretty much the only dancer in the group and a lot of them were musicians. We became not just friends, but family. We took several road trips together; one of these was to the Awaken The Dawn gathering at the National Mall in October 2018 for four days. We witnessed prayer, worship, and intercession in 50 tents representing the 50 states. It was a worship procession bringing the ark of the presence of God in the center of our nation. I remember dancing as a form of intercession in every tent. I loved seeing hundreds of musicians and singers worshipping Jesus in these tents day and night. When Awaken the Dawn was over, we headed back on the road to Pasadena, California.

During the time in California, I filled different job applications trying to find a job that would provide my living expenses. I worked at Roscoes Chicken and Waffles cleaning dishes, pots, and pans in the kitchen. The Lord was using this job to work on my character, humility, and perseverance. He taught me that character comes before gifting, which was a lesson I needed to learn because most of my life I was doing the opposite, operating in gifting before character. I knew that this season was to be molded and shaped to walk in character in all areas of my life. I knew that Jesus was King and yet He still washed the feet of His disciples. He served, and serving is being Christ-like. I got to witness at my job and share Jesus with them. I also learned to not complain on the job but to shine and be like Christ.

Roscoes Chicken and Waffles was not my only job. I was also filming a prophetic class in Glendale, California, each week for my friend Gershom and doing side film gigs. The Lord had connected me with my friend Niquio Benjo Valcobero, who is an amazingly gifted worship leader that travels the world. I would film and edit his music videos and take professional photos for him each month. So, all of these jobs were a blessing from the Lord to be on my feet paying rent and food and living in California.

One day, my leader Mando gave me the unexpected announcement that the school was planning a trip to Thailand for a month for a missions trip. He shared that I was going to be part of that trip and that the Lord would provide. I literally laughed due to my lack of faith. The school offered a partnership development class every week, taught by one of the other amazing leaders, Jeff Mott, to train the students on how to write vision letters to send to our partners. The class accomplished its goal; I was able to raise over $2,500 for this trip. The Lord did provide!

In Thailand, I filmed a short but powerful documentary. Students and teachers had the privilege to work with Thai Pastors and lead worship and prayer. Our time with these Thai Pastors at their churches greatly encouraged them, and their flames for the love of Jesus grew stronger.

During the trip, we had the opportunity to go to a small village and share the love of Jesus with these kids. We got to sing with them in worship, share testimonies, and play games with them. I was blessed to minister to them through dance and to teach them some dance moves. The most precious moment was when I saw them outside on a hot day kneeling down in a row washing the dishes in the buckets after we had a delicious meal. These kids were content living in a village and learned to serve and love each other well. Another unforgettable highlight of this trip was going to a refugee camp; a Pakistani man came to us asking us to meet his family. We had poster cards and used them to write scriptures, prophetic words and draw and color beautiful pictures to give to them. When Jesus mentions in *Mathew 25:43, "I was a stranger and you did not invite me in, I needed clothes and you did not clothe me, I was sick and in prison and you did not look after me,"* it reminded me that Jesus was happy that we visited this family in prison, for this is what we did for this man. We got to eat with this Pakistani family and pray together. It was a glorious moment which I will remember forever. After our journey ended in Thailand, we flew back to California.

While attending Ekballo, I also attended and became part of Expression 58 Church in Glendale, California. I didn't know that Shawn Bolz had been the Senior Pastor of this congregation when I started attending. One day, I had the wonderful surprise of seeing him preach. This man has a highly defined and anointed prophetic gift through which he hears from the

Lord with clarity and precision. I had met him a couple of years prior at the Firestorm conference in Harrisburg, PA, where he gave me a prophetic word by picking me from the crowd and asking me if I was a dancer. He asked, "Chris, are you a dancer? You are like a legit dancer, he's the real deal. God, I pray right now... Lord, I see that he's a Renaissance man that has been giving himself over to Your heart and Your love. So that he can be prepared for this and it's totally untraditional for the industry he's going into. The Lord said, 'I have made you to be seen and heard.' You're going to meet a lot of your spiritual heroes because you're going to be like them. You're a hero, and it will manifest. Bless you, wow!"

This blessed me immensely. So I built a friendship with him over Facebook and sent him a couple of my dance videos. Also, the worship in this particular church was like being in Heaven; although I did not have a lot of room to dance, it didn't matter. The important thing was to worship and adore my King with my dance.

Los Angeles is considered the Capitol of Creativity. I wanted to personally meet many talented artists I had been following on social media platforms, who like me were spending time in this part of the country to develop their creative gifting. My desire was to learn, share, and collaborate with them. I was able to do this with quite a few of them. I noticed that many dancers in this area of the country seem to have a relationship with their creative gift but not with their Creator. So, my objective was not to just collaborate with these other dancers, but to encourage them to connect with the Creator of their gift. I prayed for those that allowed me to, shared my testimony, and planted a seed that God could water in the proper time.

I love fashion! When I was in Jersey, I came across this website, www.yoggx.com. which sells unique clothing I have never seen before. I was really captivated by the different clothing pieces, so I decided to buy a red button-up shirt that had a samurai style to it. I was also motivated to connect with the designer of the brand, Colin Hornett. I gave him a call and shared with him my desire to collaborate with him during my stay in California; he was equally excited. We met up in Venice, had breakfast, and kicked it off. Colin Hornett was one of the most laid-back creatives I have ever met; we just clicked and it turned into a brotherhood.

He told me about this launch of C7 that he wanted me to be a part of and I was excited to be part of this movement. A high-lighted moment was when I linked up with him in Malibu. We were doing a promotional video/photo shoot for the new launch of C7, and the scenery was so alluring, I felt I was on top of the world. A lot of dancers showed up; they all had their own unique individual styles and we all got to dance and just have fun vibing together. We all came together for unity, and it was such a powerful display of love. There was a scene where this girl wore a butterfly jacket, another guy wore a leopard outfit, and others had crush velvet roses imprinted on their outfits, and they all danced together in unison. It looked like Heaven crashing down on earth and being orchestrated by God. This is why I love the beauty of creativity: no egos, no hidden agendas, just collaborating to make a thought become tangible in a unique way to share to the world.

California is the birth place of creativity
Where we use all of our artistic abilities

People from all walks of the human race
Fill up a creative space

Where thousands of Creatives are found
If you just look around

So collaboration is key
For you and for me

Creating is reflecting
Innovating and connecting

Our souls are an expression
Beyond our comprehension

Knowing you are leaving a trail
To create is to risk and sometimes fail

Your life is a masterpiece
What will you release?

We must take action when we create
If we want to level up and elevate

We create from our soul

Our thoughts have wings that begin to unfold

We are dreamers that dream
Works of art to the extreme

This world we live in is about mystery
To uncover our God-given destiny

To create
and appreciate

All that is here
Our creative vision becomes clear

"Mime makes the invisible, visible and the visible, invisible."

- **MARCEL MARCEAU**

IN 1972, ROBERT SHIELDS AND LORENE YARNELL FORMED AN American mime team that created a series of skits called "The Clinkers" in which they acted as robots. They used various individual, deliberate motions—as opposed to normal smooth motion—that are stereotypical of robots and early animatronics, enhanced by their ability to refrain from blinking their eyes for long stretches of time.

I remember watching their breakfast show on YouTube and enjoying their incredible performance skit in a kitchen where they acted as though they were robots trying to perform normal tasks. Shields was dressed in a burgundy and black robe, hair slicked back, and a wooden pipe in his mouth. He was doing these unreal mechanical moves and looked and moved exactly like a robot. His wife Yarnell had a light blue robe on with hair rollers in her hair. Her face looked like it was frozen with wonder and awe. They had breakfast together, but not in a normal human way. Cereal was poured all over with orange juice spilling on their clothes. Then, Yarnell's face would fall in her cereal bowl, and they both would fall like mannequins while the table collapsed. Their performances totally inspired me to pursue learning how to dance like a robot.

Shields and Yarnell
Have stories to tell

Eyes not blinking
Creative thoughts linking

Moving in motion
Like the ocean

Walking
Not talking

Expressing
Not Impressing

Always in character
Bringing so much laughter

They bring joy to me
To dance so free

11 / THE GLORYBOT

GLORYBOT (NOUN): A ROBOT THAT
CARRIES THE GLORY OF GOD

"The glory of God always comes at the sacrifice of self."

- *AIDEN WILSON TOZER*

In August 2019, Jaja Vankova was teaching a three-day Dance Intensive course in Seattle, WA, which I attended. I learned a great deal of body control techniques and drills, robot foundations, and basics. Three days were not enough for me; I needed to learn more, so I bought her online body control dance classes on Vimeo and started training more at home in my room. I also purchased weights for my hands and a weight vest to strengthen my technique in the robot dance.

One of the most important lessons of the robot dance I have learned was the dime stop, in which a part of my body comes to a complete sharp stop. Another lesson is tensing all my muscles in the body, so that when I dance, I look more fine-tuned and have great control of my movements. This dance was not easy to learn because it required continuous drilling of these techniques in daily practice and passionate dedication. My goal is to master the techniques of the robot dance, and to do it for the glory of God.

The word "glory" popped in my mind; I believe the Lord was showing me to use this word with "robot" and create "Glorybot," which describes who I become when I'm dancing this type of dance for His glory. Glory means God's presence, and I know His presence is always with me. So why not use my movement to fashion His presence in a unique way to the world? I have been a Glorybot everywhere I go: in malls, food places, churches, and the streets. I have had so much joy being a Glorybot and bringing that joy to others. People's expressions are priceless; they begin to smile or laugh. Joy is one of the fruits of the Holy Spirit. As a Glorybot, I get to grab people's attention and share the gospel of Jesus with them.

"Jesus called out to them and said, 'Come and follow me, and I will transform you into men who catch people for God.' Immediately they dropped their nets and left everything behind to follow Jesus."
—Matthew 4:19

This is exactly what I'm doing; the dance is the fishing rod, I am a fisher of men, and the net is my dancing. We must think of different ways to share the gospel and share Christ with people so that they get to experience new life in Him and switch eternities.

One night after worshipping at Resting Place House of Prayer, my friends and I went to Applebee's. After the meal, I wanted to dance by the entrance. There was a group of young kids standing by that area, and they immediately took out their phones and started recording me. Laughter filled the atmosphere. After I danced, I got to share my testimony with them and share the gospel. We broke into small groups and prayed for them; it was so beautiful and they got touched. A seed was planted, which the Lord would water. Kids bring me great joy; I love dancing for them and seeing their priceless expressions. They can't believe that I really look like a robot.

I am The Glorybot

With the purpose
Of carrying God's presence
Using movement for His service
Dancing for the King in Heaven

With robotic hands
Unlocking God's plan

I isolate my body
Moving mechanically

Making people smile
Bringing joy all around
Dancing with style
More animated than a clown

Not looking real
But fake
I am The Glorybot
And definitely need a break

12 / BAYMAX THE ROBOT

"Flying makes me a better care provider."

- *BAYMAX*

RECENTLY, THE LORD GAVE ME A DREAM; IN THE DREAM, I remember seeing a movie theatre, and it had the words "Big Hero 6." Once I woke up, I Googled the words and found out that they referred to a 2014 movie, which was about a 14-year-old robotics prodigy, named Hiro Hamada, who had the mind of a genius. His big brother Tadeshi inspired him to put his brain to the test in a quest to gain admission to the San Fransokyo Institute of Technology. When a tragic event changes everything, Hiro turns to a robot named Baymax, and they formed an unbreakable bond. Disney's short synopsis states,

"Baymax cares. That's what he was designed to do. Conceived and built by Tadashi Hamada, Baymax just might revolutionize the healthcare industry. But to Hiro, the nurturing, guileless bot turns out to be more than what he was built for — he's a hero, and quite possibly Hiro's closest friend." [1]

Once I read that description of the movie, I knew the Lord was speaking to me; the characteristics of Baymax were of a patient caregiver. The robot is prophetic. He can tell people's emotions: happy or sad. His colors were also very symbolic. He wore a red armor, a color that is usually related to love. Baymax was a white robot; this color usually represents purity and Holy presence, such as the Holy Spirit. My favorite line in the movie from Baymax was, "I will always be with you." These words brought comfort to my soul; for an animation movie, I was deeply touched in a powerful way. It reminded me that the Lord speaks to me and gives me discernment of people's emotions; I am also called to love.

Baymax in his caring nature represents to me the Holy Spirit, who lives in me. He is my best friend who will always be with me. Life is an adventure with the Holy Spirit. I am to be kind to others and help others see their value, purpose, and destiny in Christ. The young boy had his struggles in life but knew he had purpose, potential, and destiny. Seeing life in a new perspective is key. Baymax was a hero in this animated reality. The Holy Spirit is the true hero of all reality.

A robot named Baymax
Lays down the facts
A hero
Not a zero
Nurturing others
Being a lover
He's a friend
Till the end
He's a comforter
And a wonderer
A hero to the lost
Laying his life down no matter the cost

13 / KRUMP

"Be real in every movement, every feeling, every groove, krump with your heart, don't think, use your soul."

– THZ STORM

IT IS SOMETIMES SPELLED K.R.U.M.P., WHICH IS AN ACRONYM for Kingdom Radically Uplifted Mighty Praise, presenting krumping as a faith-based artform. Krump was created by two dancers: Ceasare "Tight Eyez" Willis, and Jo'Artis "Big Mijo" Ratti in South Central, Los Angeles during the early 2000s.

"Krump is a Street Dance popularized in the United States, characterized by free, expressive, exaggerated, and highly energetic movement. The youths who started 'KRUMP' saw the dance as a way for them to escape gang life and 'to express raw emotions in a powerful but non-violent way.'"[1]

One night, I was searching for krumpers on YouTube and came across a video of a young man Krumping for God to the song "Oceans" by Hillsong. His 10-minute dance was majestic and beautiful as it glorified God and brought tears to my eyes. This dance created a desire in me to want to learn how to krump.

Afterwards, I came across dance lessons taught online by Steezy Studio based out of Los Angeles, California, and I took some. Later, I looked up a well-known dancer that was one of the best krumpers in the world, Sherwin Salonga, known as "Beast" a.k.a "Baby Tight Eyez." I found out that he offered krump lessons, which I purchased and started practicing immediately in my room. He taught on the stances, stomps, chest, arms, gestures, and freestyle. He is not just a great dancer, he is a great human being, too. He actually is a follower of Jesus, which is amazing. God has given him a special gift to dance, and it was an honor to learn from him even from a distance. I pray I would meet him someday and be able to learn from him in person. That would be one of my dreams come true.

Sherwin paints us a picture through this message, Krump is a tool of how great we can be in real life. The way we ask others on how to improve, then practice it until we get it down, should motivate us to do the same in real life. We know we will never be perfect in dance, but we strive to be better; same with life. We know that we have strengths and we have weaknesses. We make mistakes and have to face them head on and try again. We look for mentors, big homies, and guidance; same in life. If we spend as much time and energy we do improving as a dancer, imagine if we try to improve ourselves as a human being. We can make a change with ourselves and with others.

I was hungry to learn more about dancing the krump style, so I came across www.krump.online that offered videos to learn how to krump. It had close to 50 videos from various amazing krump instructors. The owner of the site was J. Slam from Odessa, Ukraine, who is also a dancer. He spoke Russian and Ukrainian, but he offered mostly all of the courses in English. He was a great teacher and suggested practicing daily and repeatedly. I followed his advice diligently and got great results with his technique. My determination and passion compelled me to learn and perfect this beautiful craft.

Later, I attended a krump freestyle session in New York City for the first time at EXPG Studio. It was a fantastic experience! The krumpers danced inside the cypher, expressing their emotions as if the music was moving their souls. This created an energetic atmosphere that was unbelievable. After a dancer hopped out of the circle, I went in confidently and just let go. I felt one with the music, expressing myself as a paintbrush moving across the canvas. I was hearing them cheer me on, and the energy soared through me with great intensity. It was a time for me to experiment and give it my all. I was dancing, flowing from one movement to the next. This was truly an unforget-table moment in my journey through dance.

The time came to perform this style while ministering through dance at the 2019 Christmas Banquet at Resting Place House of Prayer. Ali Ferrell, the director, asked me to do a solo dance, to which I said yes. Ali would always tell me that he loves watching me dance; so, it was tremendously special to hear these words from him because he is a man of God I highly admire. After discussing it many times, the choice of the song was "Peace" by Amanda Cooke. To prepare for this special performance, I was listening to this song on replay for days on end and practiced at all hours as the Lord led me.

Before I started dancing the night of the banquet, I was feeling God's presence, a heavenly rush of God's glory running through my body. So, when I started to move my body to the music, I really felt the energy of the music. I was not just dancing, but storytelling through movement. I expressed each move with creativity, conviction, and intention. When the music built up to the climax, I started moving faster to the music. I was in a world at that moment that just felt supernatural. The crowd was cheering and the energy just kept building. The song was coming to an end, and I gracefully went on my knees, put my hands on my chest, then on my eyes. The lights shut off and the people clapped. It was such a glorious night, and I know the Lord was watching me with a smile on His face as I worshipped Him in spirit and in truth.

This experience and the creation of krump leads me to believe that this style of dance was created for the glory of God. Krump brings people together in unity. When krumpers dance, they express their unique life story through their emotions of life. The expression is beyond and people feel it.

I express myself through krump
It makes my heart pump

The expression is electric
I feel so connected

Feeling the presence of the Lord
I swing my arms like swords

Blood flowing through my veins
The Holy Spirit reigns

The tension of my movement
Moving from moment to moment

I'm creating stories with my temple
Writing in the air like a pencil

Created to create
Each motion declares, "The Lord is great"

"Jesus is heaven's alabaster jar, broken and poured out for you!"

– *ANNE GRAHAM LOTZ*

•

LIKE MARY, I HAVE CHOSEN TO POUR OUT MY EXTRAVAGANT worship through movement, using my body as if it was an alabaster jar breaking at Jesus' feet. After years of putting in time dancing as if it was precious oil being poured in a jar, my greatest desire is to pour it all out on Jesus. This dancing gift connects me to Him in such a way that I just weep and feel His intoxicating love through my being. I am captivated and addicted to His presence, as if I have to have more and more of Him with every passing breath. I am totally aware that to remain in this place of glory, I must give Him my full attention.

> "Mary picked up an alabaster jar filled with nearly a liter of extremely rare and costly perfume—the purest extract of nard, and she anointed Jesus' feet. Then she wiped them dry with her long hair. And the fragrance of the costly oil filled the house." —John 12:3

Adoration to the Lord through my movement is expressed louder than words and thoughts. As I begin to move this creative temple, I enter into the Holy of Holies. Oh, how sweet is the inside cream filling of His beautiful presence. Minutes turn into hours and time begins to transcend. It is as if I'm dancing with angels before an audience of One, as the Lord delights in me while I dance for Him. His presence moves my soul, spirit, hands, and feet.

Addicted to the feet of Jesus
Like Mary Magdalene bowing low
I give Him, all I have, all I am, and all I know
Pouring out my worship in dance
I break open all of me
Dance is my alabaster jar
All my pieces flying to Jesus
For all eternity

"*Mary of Bethany scandalizes all those who love the work of the Lord more than the Lord of the work.*"

— ERIC GILMOUR

"*To have a heart like King David is to have a heart that always returns to God.*"

- *ABBEY PHIPPS*

A "MAVID" IS A MARY THAT IS AT JESUS' FEET AND A DAVID THAT is a man after God's own heart. We must be like Mary sitting at Jesus' feet, listening and obeying Him in complete adoration while seeking His face. And like David, we should aim to be a man or woman after God's own heart and live a life of repentance and devotion. As a revelation from His heart, I believe the Lord has put these two names together and it is what He is calling us to be. Imagine David being like Mary at Jesus' feet, dancing and pouring out his worship to the true King. What would that look like? I believe it would look like messy sweat and tears of love falling at His feet extravagantly.

> "Mary has discovered the one thing most important by choosing to sit at my feet. She is undistracted, and I won't take this privilege from her." —Luke 10:42

> "After removing him, God raised up David to be king, for God said of him, 'I have found in David, son of Jesse, a man who always pursues my heart and will accomplish all that I have destined him to do.'" —Acts 13:22

Mary has chosen the good thing, and so has David: They both gazed at Jesus! David did this by singing with not just his voice but with his body as he danced. As you read this testimony of the love of God in my life, take this as an invitation to become a Mavid and allow yourself to embark on a journey of going deeper in your personal and intimate relationship with this amazing God that created each of us so uniquely.

Mavid
Mary and David
Both works of art
After God's own heart
Mary at Jesus' feet
David dancing in the street
This is what I imagine
When my creativity turns into passion
They both chose the good thing
To be covered under His wings

16 / PRACTICING HIS PRESENCE

"The sweet sense of His presence is extremely faint at first, but if I give my attention to Him, He quickly becomes the only thing."

\- *ERIC GILMOUR*

I HAVE READ THE BOOK *PRACTICING THE PRESENCE OF GOD* BY Brother Lawrence, and it has changed my life. Brother Lawrence lived in such a radical way of loving Jesus simply by adoring Him and giving Him thanks. In his book, he narrates that he cooked an egg in the glory of God simply by looking at Jesus. He cultivated intimacy with God through life's everyday tasks. The daily mundane things he did was worship unto the Lord. The soul meets God when it acknowledges God. There is beautiful joy that is obtained by practicing God's presence.

> *"For you bring me a continual revelation of resurrection life, the path to the bliss that brings me face-to-face with you."* —Psalm 16:11

Often, we busy ourselves with daily tasks, and the inclination is to forget about the Lord. If we are not connecting with the Lord, we will not be able to hear or recognize His voice, and eventually we will feel separated from Him. I truly believe people have sin issues because they stop gazing at Jesus.

> *"Are you weary, carrying a heavy burden? Then come to me. I will refresh your life, for I am your oasis. Simply join your life with mine. Learn my ways and you'll discover that I'm gentle, humble, easy to please. You will find refreshment and rest in me. For all that I require of you will be pleasant and easy to bear."* —Matthew 11:28-30

We are to come to Him daily in our highs and our lows. Worshipping God in spirit and in truth is what He is seeking from us.

Every moment we have is an opportunity to slip into deep adoration in the presence of the living God. Practicing His presence is the ultimate goal for every believer. It's laying our crowns at His feet. Even small acts of communion with God acknowledging Him are key.

Worshipping Him with the stillness of my soul brings Him much gladness. Our souls need to be fed with His love and beauty. In every mundane moment, I strive to look at God and thank Him. When my mind wanders, I give my attention back to the Lord and totally fix myself on Him. Life should be loving God daily and thanking Him a lot. There is grace to practice His presence and the calling is to yield and submit.

Let me paint the picture of how you can practice the presence of God. (I learned this from my brother in Christ, Eric Gilmour). Take time throughout the day, no matter what you are doing, and set your heart upon Jesus randomly many times a day, every day: "Lord, I give You my attention…" And when I sense my attention is fully upon Him, I say, "… and I worship You." Even if it is for 10 seconds or 20 seconds, I hold my heart on Him and I am able to drink through adoration. "Lord, I give You all my attention and I worship You."

Loving Jesus
Is what frees us

His presence is a practice
His love is what attracts us

Deeply engaged to His heart
From my heart

I give Him my attention
with my affection

Every moment is an opportunity
For me to love Him constantly

Oh He is so amazing
I will forever be gazing

At the One who created me
To be in His presence so effortlessly

"In order for my heart to love Him constantly my heart must see Him constantly."

— **MICHAEL KOULIANOS**

THOUSANDS UPON THOUSANDS WERE LIFTING UP THE NAME OF Jesus at this strategic gathering, where the sound of worshippers shook up the place. What a glorious way to end 2019 and start 2020! It was such a historical piece of time when Heaven collided with earth as our adoration rose up within us like a sweet fragrance unto the Lord. Jesus '19 has forever wrecked me in a supernatural way, tangibly feeling God's presence, soaked in tears, and feeling the baptism of love through my body as I danced to the Lord. Nothing mattered but His beautiful presence. I remember when the cello was playing, and I was so connected to the music. It felt as if God was playing me like a string during one of the worship sessions.

A young man came over and shared with me that he was behind me watching as I danced, and he was touched by God. He said he went to the back and started dancing before the Lord and it felt amazing. He told me that he only danced for the Lord in his room, and he didn't think he could dance the way I was dancing for the Lord. It was his first time dancing in public in God's presence. That was such a precious testimony for me.

Another guy came to me and repented before me saying, "I judged you and thought it was weird the way you were dancing; but then Holy Spirit immediately convicted me. I saw a white glow around you when you were dancing and I knew it was the Holy Spirit." How amazing is God! He enjoys our heartfelt and honest intentions of love before Him, regardless of what form they take.

This last girl that came to me gave me a letter and this is what she wrote:

"Hi, I don't know your name, but I see how you dance. You dance like you are in the Lord's throne room before Him. You capture God's attention. He takes pride in your dancing.

"*Praise him with drums and dancing! Praise him with the loud, resounding clash of cymbals! Praise him with every instrument you can find!" —Psalm 150:4-5*

David, when he took back the promised land, danced and praised the Lord. Your dancing is so biblical. Dance and don't be afraid. Dance and do it with the passion you have. You have ZEAL, A HEART, A PASSION FOR THE LORD. Keep it and run with it. It's part of your ministry. May God bless you as long as you live.

With Love, Alejandra"

This melted my heart and was so thoughtfully written. Before, it was incomprehensible to me that someone would take the time to write a letter to a stranger. She demonstrated the Father's love for another person.

And the last encounter I had at Jesus '19 was when the choir was singing beautiful hymns; I walked to the side of the room, closed my eyes, and worshipped the Father. God's presence was very heavy on me; and I went to the ground, shaking and crying. I was there for a while, and then someone covered me with a yellowish gold flag. I had this sense that the Holy Spirit was covering me with His glory. Later that night, I looked up what yellow and gold means prophetically. The interpretation I found was: the presence of God, light, joy, anointing, and joyful praise.

Throughout the four days at Jesus '19, people were healed, set free, encountered by God, and gave their lives to Jesus with full surrender. I will forever remember this.

I hear the sound of the Violin
Jesus the Bridegroom King enters in

The sweet fragrance of our Master
Interrupts troubled hearts with laughter

The Glory of God filling up the place
People fall on their knees and face

Hands are reaching to the sky
As we gaze into His eyes

Being the light that pierces through darkness
We lose all consciousness

Our temples being filled with love so deep
Feels like a trance as though we are asleep

Worshipping with Thousands upon Thousands
I feel so high in the mountains

Shutting my eyelids
I begin to dance in silence

Holy Spirit is in me and on me
I feel so free

Dancing in heavenly places
In front of angels with glowing faces

The 24 elders begin to smile
Watching me for awhile

Jesus looking at me in the crowd
As I am dancing in the cloud

18 / *JESUS LOVES YOU, COME*
    LOVE HIM

"It doesn't take long to tell Jesus that you love Him."

— *ERIC GILMOUR*

GOD CREATED MANKIND IN HIS OWN IMAGE TO BE HIS SONS AND daughters who look like Him and walk in unconditional love just like He does because He is LOVE. He designed His creation to always remain in His love by maintaining a close and intimate relationship with Him. He would be their source of love and, in turn, the whole world would see the goodness of the Father overflowing through the lives of His children. Mankind would fill the earth with God's way of loving and giving of Himself and thereby subdue it.

Although this was God's plan, mankind was created with the freewill to choose. This choice was tested at the Garden of Eden where the first man and woman, Adam and Eve, were placed at Creation.

"The serpent was more clever than any of the wild animals the Lord God had made. The serpent said to the woman, 'Did God really say, "You must not eat fruit from any tree in the garden"?' The woman said to the serpent, 'We may eat fruit from the trees in the garden. But God did say, "You must not eat the fruit from the tree in the middle of the garden. Do not even touch it. If you do, you will die."' 'You will certainly not die,' the serpent said to the woman. 'God knows that when you eat fruit from that tree, you will know things you have never known before. Like God, you will be able to tell the difference between good and evil.' The woman saw that the tree's fruit was good to eat and pleasing to look at. She also saw that it would make a person wise. So she took some of the fruit and ate it. She also gave some to her husband, who was with her. And he ate it." —Genesis 3:1-6 (NIRV)

Because of man's choice, mankind lost that likeness and that closeness with his heavenly Father. Apart from a close relationship with the Father, man was reduced to living by his own feelings, thoughts, and desires—reduced to living according to the "way that seems right to man"—in essence becoming a "god" unto himself. He was reduced to needing love, affirmation, and validation; living in insecurity; and at a complete loss for who he really was and why he was on the planet in the first place. So instead of looking like God's love and image on the earth, man looked nothing like his heavenly Father. Instead of subduing, he became subdued. In a very real sense, man took the nature of God's enemy and lost connection with his true identity.

But God, in His great love for mankind, at the proper time in history, sent His Son Jesus to seek and to save that which was lost.

> *"So that those who truly believe in him will not perish but be given eternal life. For this is how much God loved the world—he gave his one and only, unique Son as a gift. So now everyone who believes in him will never perish but experience everlasting life. God did not send his Son into the world to judge and condemn the world, but to be its Savior and rescue it!" —John 3:15-17*

God sent Jesus to pay a price and make a way for man to be restored back to a life of union and communion with God. To be restored back to who man was originally created to be and to do what he was originally created to do. To have God's likeness in His children and to express through His children once again.

In my personal walk with the Lord, I experienced my own transformation from a man who lost his way from birth due to the original sin of Adam and Eve, to new life full of purpose, identity, and love. The God of Creation loves me and never gave up on me. Even more, He never stopped seeing me for who He created me to be, a son and not an orphan and wanderer. My worth was restored because of Jesus' sacrifice at the Cross of Calvary. His blood shed on that cross paid my price forever. Nothing I have ever done has made Him love me any less. And by the same token, nothing I could ever do for Him could make Him love me anymore because He already loves me with a perfect love.

I was born into a fallen, self-centered existence through my earthly father and his lineage going all the way back to Adam. But I was not created to live for self; I was created to look like my heavenly Father, to shine for Him in a broken world. When I meditate on what I was really created for and realize what Jesus did to make a way for me to be restored, it opens up a door for me to change the way I think (repent) and stop living just to please myself. It reminds me of my new life in Christ Jesus where I can go deeper in knowing the Father, the Son, and the amazing Comforter, the Holy Spirit, who leads me in to perfect truth as *John 8:11 (CEB)* states, *"If the Spirit of the one who raised Jesus from the dead lives in you, the one who raised Christ from the dead will give life to your human bodies also, through his Spirit that lives in you."*

My greatest privilege and joy is to spend time with and get to know God. He has gone to extreme lengths to make a way for me to be with Him and He delights in my company. As I yield myself to God, putting off by faith the old self-centered ways and putting on by faith the new ways I see in Christ, His grace, His power working in me to do what I cannot do for myself, molds and shapes me to be the person He created me to be: a son who is growing up to look like, see like, think like, react like Him with a wholehearted devotion so that my desires are His desires. His love is not just for me to receive but for me to become, so that as God has loved me, I might become that love to others.

In this pursuit of His perfect love, I have realized that His love is very different from the "love" I have previously known. His love has no selfish ulterior motive. It is not merely a need. It is never offended. It never fails. His love is unstoppable and unchanging. It's strong, dominating, overwhelming (in a very good way).

> *"Love is large and incredibly patient. Love is gentle and consistently kind to all. It refuses to be jealous when blessing comes to someone else. Love does not brag about one's achievements nor inflate its own importance. Love does not traffic in shame and disrespect, nor selfishly seek its own honor. Love is not easily irritated or quick to take offense. Love joyfully celebrates honesty and finds no delight in what is wrong. Love is a safe place of shelter, for it never stops believing the best for others. Love never takes failure as defeat, for it never gives up. Love never stops loving. It extends beyond the gift of prophecy, which eventually fades away. It is more enduring than tongues, which will one day fall silent. Love remains long after words of knowledge are forgotten."*
> —*1 Corinthians 13:4-8*

I'm here, along with my brothers and sisters, to fulfill our vital roles, to love Him, and to bring to full expression His heart, His will, His nature—His kingdom on the earth. I'm here because God wants to show Himself to a dying world through us, reproduce His likeness, His love in others, and fill the earth with His glory. This is not because He is insecure or in need of attention, but it is to bring mankind great benefit by experiencing His love and fall in love with Him.

This same transformation I had can be experienced by you, dear reader. The longing of God for you is real and powerful if only you choose to look. He already loves you because He created you in His image. The blood of His Son paid for your past, present, and future sins. Pastor Dan Mohler expresses this truth as follows:

In the Bible, it states, "*For God made the only one who did not know sin to become sin for us, so that we who did not know right-*

eousness might become the righteousness of God through our union with him" (2 Corinthians 5:21 The Passion Translation).

Christ took the hell that you and I deserve, now God says receive Him, believe Him, put your trust and your confidence in Him, and He will forgive your sins and will guarantee you eternity in Heaven. It's all yours and free. All you have to do is receive it. God wants you to repent and turn away from your sins and turn to Him."

Repentance is beautiful.

"The repentance (metanoia) called for throughout the Bible is a summons to a personal, absolute and ultimate unconditional surrender to God as Sovereign. Though it includes sorrow and regret, it is more than that... In repenting, one makes a complete change of direction (180° turn) toward God."[1]

You have to acknowledge your sins. To sin is to act against your conscience and the good laws of life that God has given to us and that we find in the Bible. Once you confess and receive Jesus Christ as your Lord of your life, it means you are willing to let Jesus give you a new life, not just a better one. Old things pass away; all things become new and you become a new creation. Here is an encouraging prayer to help you take this crucial step in your life:

"Dear Lord Jesus, I know that I am a sinner, and I ask for Your forgiveness. I believe You died for my sins and rose from the dead. I confess and turn from my sins and invite You to come into my heart and life. I want to trust and follow You as my Lord and Savior. Father, I did not say this prayer just to get to Heaven. I said this prayer and denied myself so I can take up my cross and follow You so You can get heaven back into me, the way You intended it to be from the beginning. You created me in Your image, after Your own likeness; to be Your image on the earth."

"But God demonstrates His own love toward us, in that while we were still sinners, Christ died for us." —Romans 5:8

Pastor Dan Mohler explains, "See yourself through the finished work of the Cross. God did not send His Son to die on the cross to forgive your sins so that someday you can go to a place called heaven. He paid a price to remove your sin, to get His identity, His nature and His Spirit back in you. In other words, it is not all about you getting to heaven, it is about getting heaven back into you. So you can become what you were intended to be from the beginning apart from sin.

He is the Lamb of God who takes away the sin of the world. Then, when we say "yea brother we are always going to sin," we miss the whole point of the power of the cross and live with a sin identity. We think our ability to sin still labels us as sinners; because we believe that, that is the fruit we produce. If He forgives me of all sin and cleanses me of all unrighteousness, what is left? Righteousness! If He forgives me of all sin, what is left?

Colossians 1 tells us that we were God's enemies, but now He has reconciled us to Himself and brought us into His presence, and we stand before Him holy, blameless and without a single fault.

So, He became what we were so we could become what He is. He was beaten beyond description. The Bible says that He was marred more than any of the sons of man. That means when they were done beating Jesus, He looked worse than any man has ever left man look. When they were done beating Jesus, you could not possibly tell who He was. There's no way. Why? Why was it so sadistic? Why did it have to be so brutal? Why did they have to beat Him again and again and again? Why couldn't they just give Him the forty minus one and legally, spiritually cover it? Why did they keep beating Him with rods and whacking Him across the head, and why did they disfigure Him? Because when sin got done with man in the garden, he didn't look anything like he was created to be. So Jesus came and lost His appearance and became what we were —disfigured—so that we could have the right to get our appearance back and have our identity restored. That is love at its finest: "I know who they really are. I'll come and take what's necessary upon me to pay the price for that thing to get off of them. I'll become what they are so that they can become what I am—a son."

Everything about the Kingdom of God is held together by this one thing, that God sees you as if you have never sinned. So, if God sees you as if you have never sinned, why would you ever see yourself for what you have done wrong? How about starting where He finished and running well? How about putting on righteousness and bearing your fruit unto holiness? You are not a person trying to get it right; you've been made right. And now the Spirit of God is upon you and you begin to walk this thing out that has come alive in your heart.

See, "The Kingdom of God is not meat or drink, it's righteousness, peace, and joy in the Holy Ghost." When you have right standing with God, you have peace with God. When you have peace with God, you have amazing joy. It's "good tidings of great joy." We're not trying to be happy people. The gospel is here. God loves us, made us in His image and redeemed what He created us to be and there's no stopping us now unless we fail to see and receive.

The God of Love
From high above

Designed His creation
To live in adoration

We are created in His image
We are made from His hands that are vintage

Molded and clayed
His reflection displayed

Looking at us through His eyes of flames
His love molds our inner frame

His breath in our lungs
Love is the reason He hung
Upon that cross
His love finds those which is lost

Jesus loves you,
Come and love Him
For His love is true

19 / JESUS IS DAZZLING

"Why do I love Him? Because He dazzles me. You need to be dazzled; it will suspend you from the consciousness of self and all your surroundings. Any situation you are in is to be dazzled by Jesus."

- ERIC GILMOUR

ERIC GILMOUR'S WORDS HAVE GREATLY IMPACTED ME FOR LIFE. He had said that God is looking for those that are dazzled by Him. To know that my Beloved is dazzling, and that He has dazzled me completely blind has also been a deeper perspective of His love for me. When I look into His eyes, everything else vanishes, and I forget everything else. When I give Him my eyes, I do not have an appetite for sin. I am so dazzled by the Lord's presence. One glimpse of Jesus will set you free and bring you into completion. He's more than anything you want or can even imagine. There is nothing in this world that is more beautiful, more alluring than the Son of God. We are to throw everything at Jesus' feet, surrendering all by His dazzling beauty.

Dazzling: To shine brilliantly. To arouse admiration by an impressive display. To overpower with light. To impress deeply, overpower, or confound with brilliance. To be so overcome with light or beauty that natural conscious is suspended.

This is a prayer to the Lord by Eric Gilmour:

Dazzle me Jesus
Dazzle me broken
Dazzle me blind
Let me see you again and again
Dazzle me Jesus

As Eric Gilmour says, "He is brightness extreme, a bleeding dream," holiness is being dazzled. I lost interest in the things of this world because I tasted something from another world, and He is Jesus. When I am worshipping the Lord, I am unaware of everything else, my surroundings, the people, and time. I am clothed in the dazzling presence of King Jesus. I will never forget how beautiful He truly is, the Beloved. We were made to gaze all our days upon His Beauty. Once again, lift your eyes and behold Your Savior!

"My beloved is dazzling, with a dark and healthy complexion, outstanding among ten thousand." —*Song of Songs 5:10*

"And while he was praying, the appearance of his face changed, and his clothes became dazzling white." —*Luke 9:29*

Imagine this, you are in your secret place with the Lord, and all of a sudden the whole room gets filled with dazzling light of the Lord's presence. You fall down on your face, and then you hear these sweet words to you from the Lord:

"Do you desire good things?

There is none good but Me.

Do you desire blessing?

Is there more blessing than Me?

Do you desire power?

Who is more powerful than Me?

Do you desire spiritual heights?

Am I not the pinnacle?

Do you desire riches?

Are they not hidden in Me?

Do you desire wisdom?

Who is more wise than Me?

Do you seek friendship?

Who's a friend like Me?

Do you desire help?

Who can help you but Me?

Do you seek joy?

I am joy.

Do you seek comfort?

I am comfort.

Do you seek peace?

I am the Prince of Peace.

Do you seek life?

Can another be life to you?

Do you seek light?

I am the light of the world.

Do you desire beauty?

Who is more beautiful than Me?"

As was said to an old Greek saint when visited by the Lord...

Dazzled beyond dazzled

Jesus shines brighter than the sun
I am blinded by His beauty

I experience bliss in His presence
As He whispers my name *Chris*
I lose all consciousness

A dream within reality
He is everything to me
Consuming everything that gets in between us
I want nothing but Jesus

"Behold, He is coming with clouds, and every eye will see Him, even they who pierced Him. And all the tribes of the earth will mourn because of Him. Even so, Amen." —Revelation 1:7 (NKJV)

"Behold, the LORD rides on a swift cloud, and will come into Egypt." —Isaiah 19:1 (NKJV)

"Then, together with them, we who are still alive and remain on the earth will be caught up in the clouds to meet the Lord in the air. Then we will be with the Lord forever." —1 Thessalonians 4:17 (NLV)

"Then they will see the Son of Man coming in clouds with great power and glory. —Mark 13:26 (NKJV)

"He wraps up the waters in His clouds, and the cloud does not burst under them." —Job 26:8 (NIV)

"Clouds and thick darkness surround Him; righteousness and justice are the foundation of His throne." —Psalm 97:2 (NIV)

"And David danced before the LORD with all his might; and David was girded with a linen ephod." —2 Samuel 6:14-17

"Then he broke through and transformed all my wailing into a whirling dance of ecstatic praise!" —Psalm 30:11

"And as the ark of the LORD came into the city of David, Michal Saul's daughter looked through a window, and saw king David leaping and dancing before the LORD; and she despised him in her heart." —2 Samuel 6:16

"Let them praise his name in the dance: let them sing praises unto him with the timbrel and harp." —Psalm 149:3

"The joy of our heart is ceased; our dance is turned into mourning." —Lamentations 5:15

"A time to weep, and a time to laugh; a time to mourn, and a time to dance." —Ecclesiastes 3:4

"Dance is the art of the soul painted on the canvas of life."

- *KEVIN PARADOX*

"Dance is the only art of which we ourselves are the stuff of which it is made."

- *TED SHAWN*

"Dancing is the loftiest, the most moving, the most beautiful of the arts, because it is not mere translation or abstraction from life; it is life itself."

- *HAVELOCK EL*

"The most valuable thing the Psalms do for me is to express the same delight in God which made David dance."

- *C.S. LEWIS*

"Dancers are the athletes of God."

- *ALBERT EINSTEIN*

"Dance is the hidden language of the soul."

- **MARTHA GRAHAM**

"If dance is a language, our sentences are only as strong as the breaths taken in between the words."

- **KEVIN PARADOX**

"I see dance being used as communication between body and soul to express what is too deep to find words."

- **RUTH ST. DENIS**

"Be grateful for the twists in the road. They teach us humility and grace. And any dancer in this life requires both."

- **MARGARET B. MOSS**

"Dance was never about movement, but intention."

- **KEVIN PARADOX**

"To watch us dance is to hear our hearts speak."

- **HOPI INDIAN SAYING**

"Dance is the movement of the universe concentrated in an individual."

– *ISADORA DUNCAN*

"Dance is meditation in movement, a walking into silence where every movement becomes prayer."

– *BERNHARD WOSIEN*

"Let this day be lost to us on which we did not dance once."

– *FRIEDRICH NIETZSCHE*

"Everything in the universe has rhythm. Everything dances."

– *MAYA ANGELOU*

"To Live is to Dance, To Dance is to Live."

– *CHARLES SCHULZ*

"I saw this dude in Time Square House of Prayer working it, man. And he can really break-dance, you know, in worship... I mean... incredible! And he was checking out before the Lord; it was a gift he had and the Lord loved it."

- BRIAN GUERIN

"Chris, are you a dancer? You are like a legit dancer, he's the real deal. God, I pray right now... Lord, I see that he's a Renaissance man that has been giving himself over to Your heart and Your love. So that he can be prepared for this and it's totally untraditional for the industry he's going into. The Lord said, 'I have made you to be seen and heard.' You're going to meet a lot of your spiritual heroes because you're going to be like them. You're a hero, and it will manifest. Bless you, wow!"

- SHAWN BOLZ

"The Lord says prophetic evangelism is on you strong. I see you leading. I see your life impacting atheists. I see your life impacting street kids. I see your life impacting counter-culture. I see the neo-hippie being impacted by your life. I see people that have come out of the club scene, the party scene, the LGBTQ scene... I just begin to see the Lord beginning to use you because of your sincerity, because of your heart. I heard D.L. Moody say, 'The world has yet to see what God will do with a man fully consecrated to Him.' Chris, you are going to be one of those men; you are going to be one of those! Hallelujah!"

- SEAN SMITH

Chris enjoys dancing in the cloud of God's presence, experiencing His love and bringing to the church innovation and creativity through the creative arts of artistic movement, whether it be freestyle or choreographed. He loves to share his unique gift to the world and witness to the lost with the love of Christ.

NOTES

12. BAYMAX THE ROBOT

1. https://movies.disney.com/big-hero-6/characters

13. KRUMP

1. https://en.wikipedia.org/wiki/Krumping

18. JESUS LOVES YOU, COME LOVE HIM

1. https://en.wikipedia.org/wiki/Repentance

Made in the USA
Middletown, DE
09 June 2020